ETCHINGS
ON MY MIND

ETCHINGS
ON MY MIND

PERILS OF LIFE AND CHANGING TIMES

MARY BROCK

ISBN: 978-1-64826-539-6   (Paperback Edition)
ISBN: 978-1-64826-540-2   (Hardcover Edition)
ISBN: 978-1-64826-537-2   (E-book Edition)

Book Ordering Information

Phone Number: 347-901-4929 or 347-901-4920
Email: info@globalsummithouse.com
Global Summit House
www.globalsummithouse.com

Printed in the United States of America

"The World I Face Today!!"

THE WORLD I FACE TODAY

As I peer through my window,
At the world I face today;
I see more shadows and more darkness,
Than I ever could convey.

I see sons turn on their fathers,
And too, some mothers do seduce.
I see fathers yearn for daughters,
And some daughters do abuse.

I see much jealousy and hatred,
In so many people's eyes,
To the point where they don't try,
To place their feelings in disguise.

There's much distrust and little confidence,
Shown toward people of today;
And the sad part is it's warranted,
In this "Dog Eat Dog" world way.

There's much death and constant violence,
And so little love is shown.
In this crowded world one tends to feel,
So cold, and all alone.

DEDICATION

This book of poems of life is dedicated to my son and daughter, Quinton and LaShun. They, along with many other young people whose paths I've had the occasion to cross inspired many of the thoughts and concerns shared in my poetry, through their verbal and emotional reactions to me, their families, and others. I am feeling, and have always felt my children's growing pains; as most parents do. I'm hoping they, and other young people will realize that their parents understand them much more than they imagine.

Through the vast variety of perils of life and emotional in-sight which I have of children today, I felt the need to relay to them through the depth of my love for them, that we, as parents, are very much effected by their experiences in finding themselves and adapting to life as it is today.

I am also attempting, through my poetry, to let my children know that I am aware of the emotional changes they have gone through and are probably currently experiencing. Also, through this book, I hope to have other young people and adults realize the direct and indirect affects which they have on their families' lives. It is only then that they will know the frustration felt by parents when their child is subjected to the perils of life, and outside negative influences; and see years of teaching, protecting, and nurturing go "down the drain".

I'm hoping my children and other young people take the time to read the poems in this book, and perhaps if they honestly see themselves in the situations depicted, look at life in a different perspective from then on. I'm also hoping that they, and others will take the initiative to be responsible for making their lives worthwhile and fulfilling; and see parents as confidants, instead of adversaries.

PREFACE

This book of poetry was designed to be both educational and in-spirational, to people of all ages. However, I have hopes of reaching many young people, and preventing or resolving some of the problems which they find themselves experiencing today; those problems which ruin the rest of their lives.

I have attempted to outline the many major perils of life, which influence our young people today: at home, at school, and in society. We hear about these things in bits and pieces throughout life. Sometimes it is much too late when the child realizes these important facts of life. Many of our children can benefit from this collection of poems.

Most of the poems in this book are lengthy. I felt that there was much to say about each topic; and there is a moral to each poem. I have broken the topics down into four categories.

The first category, *"CHANGING TIME"*, contains views of time and phases of life today. The second category, *"PERILS OF LIFE"*, depicts the various perils which affect us as individuals, both young and old. It addresses current issues. The third category, *"WORD TO THE WISE"*, is intended as a self-development tool. These things will make our youths less vulnerable and less destructive. They will also establish or enhance self-esteem. The fourth category, *"WORDS OF CONSOLATION"*, will create an inner peace; sometimes with a touch of humor. This category expresses love, faith, and appreciation.

I hope our educational system will find it feasible and beneficial to include this book among the many which are used in schools and read by our children today. Though it is small in size, the rewards are great; and will be reflected in our future adults. We need to use every resource possible, to reach our children today. This is one way of getting them to address current issues and take a look at themselves at the same time. I believe this book to be a very unique collection of poetry. I hope the reader and/or someone close to them finds some benefit and enjoyment in the traditional poetry contained in this publication. I find the reading of these poems very consoling and relaxing when I am depressed, stressed, or just need some uplifting. *Happy Reading*

CONTENTS

III. WORD TO THE WISE

IV. WORDS OF CONSOLATION

A MOTHER'S LOVE

A Mother's Love, unlike the seasons,
Doesn't change when there's no sun.
A Mother's Love - She needs no reason,
To express it to someone.

A Mother's Love never digresses;
Though to you, it sometimes seems;
It's no longer there, and takes recesses;
She sees you in her thoughts and dreams.

You can depend upon A Mother's Love,
To outlast trials and tribulations;
To be God-sent from up above;
To be a strong configuration.

A Mother's love endures the pain...
The pains of which you often feel.
It brings you sunshine when it rains,
And yet, *her* pain, she still conceals.

If you ever doubt A Mother's Love,
Just think of all of your demands;
And stresses you've caused her through her love;
And yet, she stands with outstretched hands.

A Mother's Love has no boundaries;
No tests or thin lines to cross.
It's not determined by the kind of person you are...
So, Whatever you are - *her love's not lost.*

Changing Times

CHANGING TIMES

Sometimes in our minds, we relive our past...
Over and over again.
A broken heart, a growing pain,
Seems harder and harder to mend.

It seems that peace has no refuge in mind...
And past abuse has no end.
It seems that my heart forever marks time;
My subconscious will never bend.

You wonder and ponder that which may have been,
And that which you secretly know.
You often wonder how you traveled the path,
And exactly how far you can go.

There are times when you'll just stand and mark time,
Because the time you are in goes too fast.
No desire to catch up to the pace of these times;
Can't slow down, for the fear you'll not last.

A POET

A poet is someone with something to say;
Who expresses deep feelings, with hopes to convey,
A message to the world today.

A poet's thoughts come from deep within;
In hopes that some hearts and attention she'll win;
In hopes that she'll save someone some distress;
In hopes to seat morals which are bound to transgress.

A poet is someone who opens the mind;
Who relaxes the tensions which constantly bind,
Both young and old, whose refuge they find.

A poet is filled with much love and devotion,
Which is shared with the world as she gets a notion.

So, if you should meet a poet some day;
Just nod and smile gently... you're bound to convey
Your kind thoughts unspoken...
Then have a good day.

WHAT IS A MOTHER TO DO?

What is a mother to do,
When the child she raised goes in opposite ways,
From the morals she taught as he grew?

What does she do when she loses control,
When the child doesn't hear all the things that he's told,
And those morals are considered age old?
What does she do,

When the path that he takes has no end...
Or is leading to his self-destruction;
When friends are his guides and his feelings he hides,
And she sees him through so much corruption?

What does she do,
When the child that she bore is not hers anymore,
But an independent misguided missile;
That is bound to make contact with a detonating spear,
With the devastating impact she feared?

What does she do,
When the child that she knew no longer exists deep inside;
When his feelings have changed, and thoughts rearranged,
And morals replaced by his pride?

What can she do when values are few,
And he sometimes has no values at all;
When he struggles with life's most dangerous perils,
And resists the kind gestures from all?

What can she do, when his future looks grim,
And soon real friends he has not any?
She sits with her arms still stretched out toward him,
And prays that God's graces, he'll have many;
And soon, very soon, he'll come in from the storm,
And give thanks that **HIS** patience didn't diminish.

TIME

Time is of the essence;
It decides and gives commands.
Now life's most valued possession;
It's often in great demand.

There's much to be lost,
For lack of time;
It can certainly cost,
A life, a dollar, a soul, a dime.

There's yet much to gain,
When time is right...
A new lease on life;
Success is in sight.

Time is of the essence;
But, so many fail to see,
The urgency and presence,
Of the key to destiny.

If past time, present and future,
Were considered constructively,
There'd be no time for lagging,
By so many of whom I see.

PHASES OF LIFE

Life has many phases,
In which you learn and grow.
The first phase, as an infant;
You mimic all you know.

The next phase, as a toddler;
Is one in which you show,
Your individuality,
And interests which you stow.

The third phase, as a child,
Where heroes you have many;
And curiosities aroused,
Toward the value of a penny.

The fourth phase, as a youth;
The world seems full of fun.
You fail to face reality,
And values you have none.

And then you reach adulthood,
Where things all seem to change.
You stumble into *facts of life*;
Your life is rearranged.

Through these phases there's one concern,
Which tends to be ignored.
The guidance which we need so much,
Is often not disposed.

I'M GROWN-UP NOW

I'm grown-up now, as you can see;
I'm 17, and should be set free.
I expect to come and go as I please;
It matters not, that I lose the door keys...
I'm Grown-Up Now!

I should not be made to do the chores;
Nor have to ask to go outdoors.
I should not get whippings and scoldings too;
I should not be told what to do...
I'm Grown-Up Now!

I should not be questioned as to where I go;
That's something I don't think you must know.
I will expect more money than I've been receiving,
And your old-fashioned rules, at the door I'll be leaving...
I'm Grown-Up Now!

Oh! By the way, I'll expect that you,
Will adapt to me... rather than I to you;
I'm Grown-Up Now!

I feel that I know a little more than you,
And may express myself in the manner I do.
My choice of foods has changed, as well,
As my disposition, as you can tell...
I'm Grown-Up Now!

So, save the lectures and advice;
My Love and Respect are hereby on ice...
I'm Grown-Up Now!!

WHAT EVER HAPPENED?

What ever happened to Faith and Love;
Those wonderful emotions sent from above?
Those days of old have all turned cold,
When there was much respect for the old.

What ever happened to parental affection?
It seems to have gone in the other direction.
People have changed so much through the years,
That there is an abundance of blood, sweat and tears.

What ever happened to morals and guidance?
Our children no longer see us as confidants.
They're often misguided by corrupt peers and adults,
To the point that they ignore all morals they're taught.

Whatever happened, I'm sure there's a way,
To reach all concerned about our status today.
I'm hoping our youth, with purpose unfound;
Will somehow see fit to turn this life around.

BUDGET

You know, it seems that everywhere,
There's a budget nowadays.
There seems to be more thought toward
How the profit margin sways.

Of course it's only ethical,
To budget home expenses.
If not, you'll find you're in the red,
And darn near lose your senses.

But, budget in the business world,
now takes the place of man.
It's "Make the budget, Cut the staff;
Squeeze 12 into 8 if you can.

PEOPLE

People say the strangest things,
To see if you are listening.
The things they say can make you sad;
Or make your bright eyes glisten.

People do the strangest things,
To try and draw attention.
They joke, they cry, and loudly sigh;
And more I dare not mention.

People are the strangest things;
They come in varied sizes.
The way they act from day to day;
To me, there are no surprises.

People are changing with the times;
It's self-preservation or burst.
Survival seems to be the cause;
Let's hope they don't get worse.

STRESSFUL TIMES

There are as many stepping stones in life,
As there may be stumbling blocks;
But in this day and time right now,
Seems we only feel the hard knocks.

Stress has never known a home,
As prominent as ours.
It seems that stresses build and build...
More unbearable by the hour.

Young folks can't bear the slightest strain,
Upon their inner strength.
To them, life bears them lots of pain,
And endurance has no length.

There tends to be some conflict,
Of emotional response;
Controlling physical reaction,
Which we wish to keep in bonds.

I've come to realize that stress,
Of conscious mind controls;
That of which subconsciously,
Your memory tends to hold.

THE ROOF IS ON FIRE

The roof is on fire...
If it burns the house will go.
Our future path is blocked,
Although the fire smoulders low.

The heat is in the attic,
And the past will be no more.
The fire burns much hotter,
Than it's ever burned before.

The fire is being kindled,
With more hate and lack of love.
We're hoping for a rainy day,
Sent from the Lord above.

The roof is on fire...
And no one will put it out.
I fear you'll miss the point,
Of what this poem is all about.

Perils Of Life

PERILS OF LIFE

Life is but a bed of roses,
With petals and plenty of thorns.
Life's path can be so rugged,
Or as straight as the day you were born.

It all begins with morals,
And interpretations of same;
And later you will learn;
It's how you play the game.

You first begin with childhood,
When laws and rules are made.
Like water on a duck's back,
You fail, or make the grade.

Your future depends on many things;
Your frame of mind and goals.
Life can be an empty stage,
On which you play many roles.

When you try to live as others do,
Or how they think you should;
You run into many obstacles,
Which you never dreamed you would.

There are influences on the streets,
As well as problems on the job.
There seems to be no way out;
Your heart just throbs and throbs.

The stress which you experience;
The pain of life today;
The tolls and tribulations,
Will all be changed, *I Pray.*

OBSTACLES

Obstacles were meant to be;
They serve as stepping stones.
If it were not for obstacles, you see;
We may as well be clones.

They teach us to use our judgment,
When things don't go our way;
To take alternative routes,
When plans begin to decay.

They develop your endurance;
Teach us to persevere;
Build up strong resistance
Toward the many things we fear.

If it were not for obstacles,
Our purpose would run wild.
They justify our means,
And bring forth adult from child.

WHAT DEATH IS

Death is just a state of being;
A state of rest...
A state of peacefulness.

I view not death full of sorrow;
It's merely an extension...
Extension into tomorrow.

When one has lived in this restless world;
The peace of death,
Seems life unfurled.

I know not now, the pain and sorrow;
Called forth yesterday...
Lasting through tomorrow.

And still I smile, as though content;
My state of being
Is Heaven sent.

This poem was written in hopes of helping all who read it to
accept the loss of a loved one as an inevitable passage of life
from a worldly state to blessed eternity.

JUNGLE OUT THERE

I remember when Mama used to say,
"It's a jungle out there"... in no uncertain way.
She used to warn me all about,
The world out there - It's cold throughout.

She'd tell me, "There are people who
Have no concern about such as you".
There are those who will befriend you;
But, watch your back, is what you must do.
It's a jungle out there!

No matter how strong you think you are,
Someone out there will influence you by far.
They'll set your confidence ajar;
Your pre-taught morals, soon they'll mar.
It's a jungle out there!

You must bear your burdens all alone,
Because the people out there...
They bear their own.
You must make sound decisions on your own,
Or be ready to suffer consequences known.
It's a jungle out there!

There are things out there that you don't expect;
So keep both eyes open, and your head erect.
There are so many who do evil deeds,
Because they're only concerned with their own needs...

And most of all, *keep Love in your heart*,
Because staying on your feet has become a true art.
It's a jungle out there.

In spite of all the perils and strife;
Remember your morals... the key to your life.
So take this advice before you ascend,
The staircase of life, you'll soon comprehend.
IT'S A JUNGLE OUT THERE!

MONEY

Money seems to motivate,
The people of today.
It's the root of all evil,
And many people pay.

The value of a life is set,
According to ambition;
And how much you can profit,
With less thought of admonition.

Money changes people's,
Personalities and moods;
And need I speak of attitudes
Toward others they abuse?

Money seems to be the force,
Which guides the human hand.
It guides our thoughts and actions too;
It's always in demand.

But, what if money were to change,
Its value, and be worthless?
Would we still be destruction bound;
And would life be as ruthless?

CRIME

Crime is like a snowball;
It gets bigger all the time.
At first it's childish pranks,
Then it's juvenile spare time...
And from there to major crime.

The tolls of crime may vary,
From one to ninety-nine.
Though the situations vary;
You're bound to tow the line.

Crime has no emotions;
Nor afterthoughts, it seems.
It seems to be done by notions;
By singles and by teams.

The rewards of crime are phantom;
Though great it seems to many.
You'll find there is a ransom...
You'll pay down to the penny.

Crime seems to draw more youths today;
If they only knew what price they'll pay;
They'd change their course of life's highway,
And prevent the future scars... *Today.*

DRUGS

I wonder if they really see,
What Drugs can do to them?
I'm sure they hear the daily news;
Yet, use Drugs at every whim.

I wonder what it takes,
To make them see that Drugs Are Bad?
The way they self-inflict their pain;
It makes me very sad.

Drugs are called narcotics,
Which tend to ease the pains;
But what about the other things,
That they do to human brains?

Drugs will induce sleep;
Bring on a stupor, coma, or death.
They suspend or deaden sensibility;
Numb awareness and ruin your health.

The saddest part of all is that,
The relief which they are seeking,
Is only temporary...
So, the Drugs keep right on leaking.

And once they hook themselves on
Drugs, A life of crime begins;
Because the habit is so deadly,
Their life quite often ends.

POLITICS

Politics is nothing but,
A way to sell your soul.
You cast aside all morals taught,
To accelerate your goal.

There is private politics,
And public politics, as well.
It makes no difference which;
Your soul is what you sell.

You sell your soul to buy some time;
For which you'll pay a plenty;
But, watch your step, for soon you'll find;
Your self-respect, not any.

Then further down the line you'll find,
You've lost more than you knew.
Your underhanded deeds, it seems;
Will be your downfall too.

Those same tactics which you used,
Will serve as stepping stones,
To others whom you did abuse,
By unjust deeds unknown.

THE HOUSE OF CORRECTION

This place that they call "The House of Correction",
Where even inmates are in need of protection...
The conditions and omissions always in the news;
This House of Correction, so-called in *their* views.

And now that I'm here, I finally see;
This place is the pits... I can't even be me.
I have to accept what the officers do,
Or be prepared to fight the whole darn crew.

Each day is routine, no matter how long you're here;
And the space that I have is minute, as I peer
At the long row of cells on the opposite side;
I fear for my life, but there's no place to hide.

As I wonder and ponder what has happened to me,
I see inmates grow colder... and more violence I see;
And I know well, what I must do to survive,
This city of HELL... *God, I must stay alive.*

THE HOUSE OF CORRECTION . . .

There are inmates here, doing one to ninety-nine,
That do all that they can to elongate your time.
It's so hard to stay cool and unbiased in here;
Either you're into a "click", or for your life you fear.

I thought I was cool when I followed the crowd;
And the crowd's all here, but not talking so loud.
For in here they all found someone tougher than they...
In here, you must definitely watch what you say.

I've had time to review well, my life through the years,
And I suddenly find myself fighting the tears.
I came up with the view of the mess that I've made,
Of *my* life, and the loved ones whose love I still page.

God, if only you'll grant me a chance to amend,
My posture and lifestyle, I surely will mend,
All the damage I've done to myself and my friends...
And my family I'll cherish and love to no end.

SILENT WAR

There's a silent war going on it seems;
The cause is not yet clear.
I don't know what it all means...
I'm too far away to hear.

But, I do know it's been going on,
For quite a long long time.
I just haven't stopped to ask myself,
If I could be more kind.

It will only take a little time,
To find out just what's wrong;
And what it is that causes us,
To never get along.

Each time I think it's over,
It starts right up again.
I'm going to try and do my best,
To end it if I can.

MISUNDERSTOOD

Why am I so misunderstood?
I guess nothing ever turns out
Like I'm told it should.

I try real hard to lend a hand,
But it seems to many others...
That's not what I planned.

I do my best to share the things,
Which I have learned with others...
But scorn is all it brings.

I always make an effort to
Do the best job that I can...
But, to some my best won't do.

Why am I so misunderstood?
Perhaps it's how I express myself...
Or how *they* think I should.

Whatever the reason I'm misunderstood;
I pray God forgives them,
As I know he would.

SILENT CRY

As I walk the streets... *so COLD*,
I shed a tear with every step.
It seems that everywhere I go,
The silent cries of theirs are kept.

So, silently I cry, as the trail of tears run deep,
As I discern the many faces,
I cannot help but sigh and weep.

The faces of the many children,
That have not and never will;
The youth and young adults, all street-bound;
Whose destinies are unfulfilled.

As they reach for what they think,
Soon might become a "Shooting Star",
With no idea of what they're doing,
And how destruction-bound they are.

So, silently I cry, as the trail of tears run deep,
As I discern the older faces,
I cannot help but sigh and weep.

The faces of the many elderly,
And the homeless on the streets;
These faces often are forgotten,
Yet, in the past they were all concrete.

If we would just reach out and touch,
The many faces that we see;
And show a bit of understanding,
Concern, and Love for those we meet.

So, silently I cry, as the trail of tears run deep,
As I pass the many faces,
In them somehow I see *you* or *me*...
And cannot help but sigh and weep.

WHEN JUSTICE HAS NO COLOR

I look forward to the day,
When justice has no color;
When all are treated equally,
True justice they'll discover.

Ever since I can remember,
It's been rendered on a scale.
It depends on your defenses,
Whether justice will prevail.

It depends on ability to pay,
And this is what I mean...
You seem to get a better break,
When you have more of *"the green"*.

But some are not as fortunate;
This color does control...
The way we live, the way we feel;
It stops the wheels of justice cold.

MAMA'S UNSELFISH LOVE

I wish Mama wouldn't fuss so much,
Or spank me when I'm bad.
She takes all the fun from life,
And it makes me really mad.

I wish she wouldn't make me eat,
All the foods that I don't like.
She doesn't like for me to waste a thing;
She makes sure I chew my food up right.

I wish she would let me stay up late,
To watch the late late show.
Besides, why does she think she's so smart;
And anyways, what does she know?

She knows if she doesn't caution me,
Or correct me when I'm wrong;
I'll keep doing the things I shouldn't,
As if they're the right things all along.

She has to discipline and control me,
And to her that's just not fun.
She has to teach me to eat my food right,
And be nice to everyone.

She knows that all the rest I get,
Will build a body big and strong.
All this Mama knows is best for me,
As she shares her love unselfishly.

Word To The Wise

OH CHILD OF FAITH

Oh Child of Faith, Oh Child of Grace;
I fear you will not keep the pace,
To gain success in this human race.

I fear that you will be consumed;
By outside influences you're doomed...
But, though the sins of the world you're spooned,
I pray that your life not be marooned.

Here's hope that knowledge you will gain;
And that you will withstand the rain;
As well as learn to ease the pain...

But if your troubles seem not to pass,
Keep the faith that you will outlast
The perils of life toward you outcast...

And even when it seems to be,
That your life will ne'r be trouble free;
Your faith in God will clear debris,
And light your path... as you will see.

Oh Child of Faith, Oh Child of Grace;
I'm confident you'll win this race,
If you approach life at a steady pace,
And remain in *HIS* good grace.

PEER PRESSURE

I often hear a phrase referred,
To youth and their aggression.
Peer pressure is the phrase I'm told,
Which causes great digression.

Peer Pressure is allowed to be,
The controlling factor only,
When young folk lack self-confidence,
And peers influence strongly.

Those who relent to Peer Pressure,
Are also showing admission,
Of weakness that's far greater than,
Those peers whom they commission.

You must maintain your voice and views,
Against all opposition.
Be assertive, and stick by morals taught;
Allow none to change your position.

So, when your peers suggest something,
Of which you are opposed;
Remember, *it takes a better man,*
To stand the grounds he chose.

YOU'RE GROWN-UP NOW

You're grown-up now, when you can see,
That your actions control your destiny;
When you realize you make mistakes;
When you know that hard work is what it takes,
To accomplish goals and dreams.

You're grown-up now, when you realize,
That others have feelings too;
When you honestly analyze,
The unethical things you do.

You're grown-up now, when you can see,
That life is not a cherry tree.
There are good times, and bad times,
And happy times, and sad times;
Which you'll endure successfully.

You're grown-up now, when you can see,
In life, you'll have responsibilities.
You'll have to take instructions from
Others, in addition to Dad and Mom.

You'll have to learn to hold your tongue;
That expressions can alter words unsung;
That with some you'll have to be discreet,
If you intend to land upon your feet.

You're grown-up now, when you realize;
These things are vital, if you're to survive,
In the world as it is today.

VALUES

This world is full of Values;
The worth of things untold.
Values differ as people do;
Like tin, and silver, and gold.

To estimate a value,
You first must have a goal.
A goal is set in childhood,
Or further down the road.

You reach the point where you may wonder,
Why toil and strife don't pay.
The dark cloud turns to thunder,
And it rains and pours each day.

Then take a look at values,
And double check your goals.
There may be need to modify
Your values and your goals.

Your goals must be affordable,
Which you can work within.
If not, you'll find much conflict,
And confusion will begin.

You can not please your Mother;
You can not please your Dad;
You must defend your own choice,
Which makes you very sad.

If only *You* would set your goals,
There would be no need for others.
Self-worth must take priority;
Then values of your brothers'.

EDUCATION

If you set great value,
In the image you portray;
Then education you must know,
Is above all else today.

Beauty is only skin deep;
But knowledge runs much deeper.
The price you pay for lack of skill,
Will end up even steeper.

It's a matter of priorities,
Which you must learn to set.
Don't let your current actions,
Be ones which you'll regret.

The skills of most careers today,
Require higher education.
So, if you're wise, you'll stay in school,
And avoid self-deprivation.

The pride which you'll experience,
From knowledge you will gain,
Is worth much more than money;
And it's sure to spare some pain.

RESPECT

Respect yourself, and others will;
Have confidence that you'll fit the bill.

Respect all others for whom they are;
And never misjudge them by far.

Respect your parents, for they know well,
The toil and strife that you'll entail.

Respect the rights of your brothers;
And in return, they will respect others.

Respect is spread in this manner;
Be proud to hold up the brotherhood banner.

PERSEVERE

P is for persistence in everything you do;

E is for effort, and extra effort too;

R is for resistence, to problems and the like;

S is for sense of judgment, in decision-making hike;

E is for efficiency, of which you must maintain;

V is for victorious, in tasks and duties gained;

E is for endeavors, and minimum of pain;

R is for reliance, upon your self-esteem;

E is for excellence, in which you wish to gleam.

DO UNTO OTHERS

Have you ever stopped to wonder why,
People treat you as they do?
It has to do with changes,
You take other people through.

Have you ever stopped to notice,
When tempers are aflare;
That your voice tone was offensive,
As your thoughts began to air?

Have you ever stopped to think,
About the things you say and do...
That you never do to others
As you wish things done to you?

As you go through life, I'm sure,
You will undoubtedly find,
That you receive that which is given;
So, for *Your* sake... *be kind.*

BRAIN-DEAD

I hear they consider me brain-dead,
Though I walk the streets day by day.
They say that this brain in my head
Is as dead as a brand new toupee...

For it fails to work when it should;
It recesses when it's in demand;
It constantly keeps me up to no good,
And it does what all others command.

Of my senses, I must take control;
My actions, I must try to guide.
Beginning today, I must set some goal,
To prove that my brain has not died.

IF I COULD JUST ACCEPT

If I could just accept myself,
As imperfect as I may be;
Perhaps I'd see as others do...
I'd see the good in me.

I'd allow the good and kind in me,
To overpower the bad.
I would radiate the joy of life,
And forget what make me sad.

If I could just accept the things,
Of which I cannot change;
My life would be much simpler;
My goals, I'd rearrange.

If I could just accept the things,
That people say to me,
To make *ME* a better person...
A *BETTER* person I'd be.

If I could just accept the change,
In people of today;
Adjust myself and rearrange,
My life along the way.

I CAN

I can forever be dependent,
Upon others for support...
Or I can be independent,
And my selfish ways abort.

I can always look to others,
To make all of my decisions...
Or I can begin to use my head,
And decide with great precision.

I can always blame someone else,
for all the mistakes I've made...
Or I can face reality,
and the truth I'll not evade.

It's plain to see what I can be,
Without putting forth an effort...
But if I'd just apply myself,
There's no limit whatsoever.

BEFORE WE SPEAK

If we would stop to think about,
What we have to say;
When we open our mouth to speak,
Kind thoughts we would convey.

Instead, our thoughts are flighty;
Our mouth cannot keep pace;
Or thoughts come out before we think,
And cause us much disgrace.

If we would just control our mouths,
And put on a happy face;
We'd choose our words and time to speak,
Use tact, and speak with grace.

But, pride will not allow us,
To escape the walls of doom;
Instead, we burrow deeper,
And the consequences loom.

THE EYES OF A FOOL

The eyes of a fool can see no wrong,
In evil deeds when done.
He sees no other way of life,
Except to hurt someone.

The eyes of a fool can never see
The things which hurt him most.
He'll blame others for his misfortune,
When it is *he* who hurts him most.

The eyes of a fool refuse to see
Life in its reality.
He never seems to be content;
All others' rights he'll circumvent.

The eyes of a fool will often shift
To temptation all around him;
But, if he ever stops to think;
He'll find, it's *he* who bounds him.

LOOK INTO THE MIRROR

Look into the mirror,
And tell me what you see.
Do you see the kind of person,
Which you really wish to be?

Do you see a face of confidence;
Someone with strong desires,
To make your life worthwhile...
One which even you admire?

Or do you see someone,
Who needs assistance from another;
Someone who's quite dependent,
Upon decisions made by others?

The way you see yourself
Is the point I'm trying to make;
That what you think of you
Decides the path that you will take.

FACTS OF LIFE

A fact of life is that it's hard;
And many say it's fair.
It separates the men from boys,
And women everywhere.

Another fact of life is that
It's what you make of it.
Though circumstances may occur,
You have to use your wit.

It is indeed a fact of life,
That things are always changing;
And you must always be prepared,
To do some rearranging.

Another fact of life, you'll find;
You reap just what you sow;
And only time will tell,
That what I've said is so.

Be not afraid to venture far,
And learn what life is all about;
But, be prepared to face the facts...
Someday your shield, you'll be without.

NOTHING IN LIFE IS FREE

Childhood is the prime of life,
When everything is free;
To many youth and children...
At least it seems to be.

But, have you ever thought about
What parents have to pay...
The sweat and tears throughout the years,
To make things seem that way?...

And when you finally do grow up,
You have the wrong perception.
It's hard to change your chain of thought;
There's hardly an exception.

And as you grow, you soon will find
That nothing in life is free.
Someone will always pay the cost;
Whether it be you... or me.

So, understand these words I say;
As you go through life you'll see;
That even though it seems that way...
Nothing In Life Is Free.

ONE DAY AT A TIME

If you live life one day at a time,
Your disappointments will be few.
If you learn to take things as they come,
You'll avoid what counting days ahead can do.

Tomorrow is never promised,
But today is always here.
When you put heart and soul in tomorrow,
Today will waste away, I fear.

It's good to work toward future goals,
But take one day at a time;
So, when obstacles obstruct your path,
Your footage you'll always find.

For when you place great store in things,
They tend to disappoint you.
The effects that disappointment brings,
Leaves scars which alter you.

So, take it slow... and learn to grow;
With each day's accomplishments you'll find;
You'll prevent more heartaches than you know,
If you take ONE DAY AT A TIME.

HUNG UP ON RIGHTS

We're so hung up on rights that we can't see,
That we all have responsibilities.

Welfare rights, prisoners' rights, the right to be free;
We'll never see the flowers, if we don't remove the tree.

We're so hung up on rights that we can't do,
What's expected of us, and required too.

Self-respect, love, and honesty are treasured by so few;
We'll never weather the storm, if we can't absorb the dew.

We're so hung up on rights that we can't feel,
When someone else is getting the raw end of the deal.

Courtesy and tactfulness, and patience always heals
The wounds of daily stresses; You'll see how great it feels.

We're so hung up on rights that we can't listen,
For valuable facts that might be missing.

Mistrial, trial by judge, trial by jury;
Newspaper, word of mouth sparks the fury.

Everyone has the right to live, the right to love, the right to be,
Whatever your heart desires, as long as you agree,
That life is what you make it...We'll soon remove the tree.

THE BEST OF A BAD SITUATION

Make the best of a bad situation;
For it will only last as long as *you* can.
The name of the game is self-preservation.
Therefore, you must have an alternate plan.

Develop your knowledge and your skills;
In order to have a bank to draw from.
So, when subjected to life's worst spills;
You'll pick yourself up... refuse to be stunned.

Make the best of a bad situation.
Tap all resources and dare to be prone,
To overcome whatever fate befalls you,
And make the impact of your presence known.

Whatever you do, remember that you
Should never give in to defeat;
To the point where you make bad matters worse,
And no longer can be discreet.

INDIVIDUALITY

I could never be the person
That you often wished I'd be;
Though I did not see at first,
That I must always be, just me.

I could never see from your eyes,
All the things that you can see;
But I can see that it's a challenge,
Getting you to see, I must be me...

You seem to never understand
Why I react the way I do,
Or why I shelter some resentment,
And lack of gratitude toward you.

If you could only see my need
For individuality;
I trust, you'll also see
That it's my first choice, to be me.

DESTRUCTION

This world is full of destruction;
The product of ignorance and pride.
The misinterpretation of some,
That the world owes them a free ride.

The sooner we understand one thing;
The better our future will look.
You reap just what you sow;
Just as it says in the "Good Book".

You may not pay right away,
For the wrongs you've done today.
When wrongs are done, you guide your path
To destruction down the way.

So each time fate befalls you;
In adulthood, or as a kid;
Take time to reevaluate,
To see just what you did.

Now I leave this thought with you,
In hopes that you will be,
A better human being,
Whose life is trouble-free.

EVIL

As I was reared, and morals taught;
Those morals seemed to guide me...
And as I grew, with love unbound;
Much evil seemed to tide me.

I was taught to hear no evil,
See no evil, speak no evil;
But evil seemed to find me.
With lots of love, and constant prayer;
No evil ever binds me...

And so I say to one and all,
When evil deeds seem to befall;
Love, faith and prayer will fix it all.

WHAT HAVE WE HERE?

What have we here?...
The world on a silver platter.
Though to some of us,
This gift doesn't seem to matter.

We've got the birds and the bees,
The flowers and the trees;
We've got the tamed and the wild,
The oxen and the deer;
Yes, all of these things are what we have here.

We've got many resources,
On which we depend;
Their benefits and uses
Just don't seem to end;
What we have here, HIS grace does descend.

We've got love, faith and charity;
A wealth of emotions;
And all kinds of freedom,
From ocean to ocean.

VENGEANCE

Vengeance is like a cancer;
It eats away at you all the time.
Until you get self-satisfaction,
You sacrifice peace of mind.

Day in, day out you're busy,
Looking forward to that day,
That you avenge your misfortune;
And make your adversary pay.

Vengeance can lead to,
A number of things;
But, self-destruction,
It only brings.

All of your energy is spent;
Your self-control will soon relent.
You soon set aside all morals taught;
Your peace of mind becomes distraught.

The moral of this poem you see,
Is that your soul is never free,
When vengeance you allow to be,
A factor of your destiny.

I WONDER WHAT I MISSED?

Now that I've grown up;
I wonder what I've missed?
The young and foolish fantasies;
The chance to make Dean's List?

I wonder if the time will come,
When I will count the hours,
I walked with much contentment,
And watched bees among the flowers?

The things which I've experienced;
The watch around my wrist;
If I could turn back the hands of time,
To see just what I missed.

These thoughts are common,
With most of us.
They haunt our minds,
And cause disgust.

It was not meant for us to relive,
Our lives once more,
Our souls to give,
To reminiscent thoughts relived.

So, when reminiscing in the past,
Be thankful that you did outlast,
The perils of yesterday.
Look on to greater things in life;
Look on to far less toil and strife;
For today begins the rest of your life.

I SEE

I see life as one big challenge;
With so many stepping stones.
I see latent opportunities,
I fear will soon be gone.

Success in life depends a lot,
On how you see it now.
Right now I see so many youths,
Who'll foul it up somehow.

I see someone who pictures life,
As one big carousel;
Someone whose growth will be deferred;
Whose life will ne'r excel.

The moral of this poem, you see;
Is life is how you see it;
And if you always see no way;
Then often... *So Be It.*

HEART, BE WISE

A few stolen hours... a stolen kiss;
To make up for the love you often miss;
But does it really fulfill your desire,
For the love you really wish to acquire?

A smile, a sigh, a gentle caress;
From your loved one, your love will digress;
And for a moment, your love will bloom;
For the dreams of a child will once again loom.

So, Heart Be Wise... and use discretion.
Be in control of your transgression.
For the weight of true love is not as flighty,
As the stolen love, you think so mighty.

DO NOT DECEIVE

I see no comfort in deceit,
As others often do.
One day our God they'll have to meet;
They'll pay the debt that's due.

It seems as though they always get,
The things they're looking for;
But, what they all seem to forget...
HE'll close some other door.

And most of all, they'll have to live,
With distrust ever on their mind;
The thought that someone, to them will do,
What they do all the time.

So keep in mind the things you do,
Will someday be returned.
Do not deceive the people who,
Show trust, though yet unearned.

WAYWARD CHILD

A child is very sensitive,
In many many ways.
With burdens he'll attempt to live;
He'll brood for days and days.

He harbors much abuse from those,
Whose love he seek to find.
For many years he keeps his thoughts,
In abeyance in his mind.

His actions are results of things,
Of which he can't express.
Sometimes his actions will impede,
His chance for happiness.

But, if you stop and think about,
Your child's real need for love;
Where love is given, it shall be returned;
So says the Lord above.

GOING NOWHERE

Forever moving, and going nowhere;
My life seems to have no direction...
And worst of all, I don't seem to care,
Enough to make needed corrections.

Forever moving along with the crowd,
And trying to keep pace with the time;
Yet, I've done nothing of which to be proud;
In my pockets, I have not a dime.

Forever moving toward my self-destruction;
At this point, I may turn around.
I pray, it's not too late for re-construction;
For my senses, I finally found.

ONE WITHOUT VALUES

I have desires, but no intentions;
I have ideas I never mention...
But worst of all, I have no goal;
Yet seldom do as I am told.

I haven't yet grown up, you know.
It's often that they tell me so;
But there is something I have learned;
Something of which I am concerned.

It took a while for *me* to see,
The person that I wish to be.
I hope that *you* will try to do,
The things you know are best for you;

Just listen to the ones who care,
And *not all others, everywhere.*

MY ACCOMPLISHMENTS?

I'm proud to say I'm one of the crowd;
At least they tell me so.
To them, I've something to be proud;
To them, I'm in the know.

But what have I accomplished now?
Somehow I fail to see.
My independent thoughts are now,
No longer part of me.

I haven't quite grown up, you see.
I dare not take control.
I haven't yet discovered me;
And still I have no goal.

My actions often domineered,
By friends of whom I knew.
It all adds up to what I feared...
My accomplishments are few.

BLACK BEAUTY

It is the name they gave a horse;
A name they thought quite fitting.
The beauty of his shiny coat...
So black, and strong, and witty.

The beauty of this horse, you see,
Made him stand out from the rest;
And every time he got the chance,
He showed them that he was best.

It seems quite strange that some can't see,
That Black's as beautiful as can be.
Our strength is known from days of old;
Why not our wit known equally?

We, ourselves are so inclined,
To use our physical strength;
While others build upon their mind,
We dig for us, a trench.

It's not enough to say we're proud.
We must excel at every chance;
And since we too stand out from the crowd;
OUR IMAGE WE MUST ENHANCE!

I'M A MAN

It's often that I seem to hear,
These words, from men both far and near;
"I'm A Man", is their excuse for things;
The things that often heartache brings.

"I'm A Man", is what they often say,
When they think things should go their way.
"I'm A Man", they feel should e'er suffice,
When their actions prove not to be so nice.

But, I'm sure most women will agree;
In these cases, it's not a *man* they see.
It's a boy who has not yet succumbed,
To being the man he must become.

I say, "I'm A Man", is no excuse,
For men's misbehavior and abuse.
When the time comes for them to pay their dues,
"I'm A Man" won't do... Their souls they'll lose.

IF I BELIEVE IN ME

I can be a shining star,
Amidst a cluster of dark clouds;
Or I can dim my light,
And commence to following the crowds.

If I maintain my stride and pride,
No matter where I go;
I'm sure to shed light upon those of whom,
Their goals seem not to know.

It matters not the place, you see...
Of where I wish to be.
What matters most is that I maintain,
My self-esteem... *for ME*.

COMMON SENSE

Here I stand...
I'm not so tall;
And perhaps I can't
Reach you at all.

From my mouth,
Comes no dictionary;
My word span may
Seem quite contrary.

To you it seems,
I have no knowledge;
Perhaps it's because,
I had no college.

But I thank God,
For common sense;
In that I didn't gain,
At your expense.

INDIVIDUAL

I am one...
I'm as individual as I can be.
The fact is...
I am in charge of my destiny.

Another fact is...
If I should somehow fail,
Or fall short...
An ill-sought destiny will prevail.

I'm an individual...
I know that Drugs are no good for me;
Cause if they were,
I strongly believe they'd be free.

Guess you know...
The best things in life are free.
That's exactly why,
I base my life upon love, hope, and prosperity.

I am individual...
Though I'm often found in a crowd.
I stand steadfast,
As I claim my individuality out loud.

NO RACE, CREED, OR COLOR

I don't see the color of your skin,
I just see the heart within;
I hear a heart that beats like mine;
A pulse that gives your vital signs.

I see someone who's equally sane,
With the same blood flowing from vein to vein.
I see someone just as proud as I,
And from his insides out - THE VERY SAME GUY.

I don't see the color of your hair or your eyes,
Because to me, they're only a means of disguise;
It's what I see far beyond them that matters to me;
They may be blonde, brown, or black...
And still IT'S *YOU* THAT I SEE.

DIFFERENCES

What causes people not to get along... DIFFERENCES!

Differences of opinion, and no compromise,
The steadfast way in which they criticise,
Will soon cause their love a latent demise.

Moral differences in each's upbringing,
Can cause a gap to slowly form;
And create a chill, where it once was warm.

Differences in sexual preferences will,
Cause them both to seem unfulfilled;
The different personalities soon,
Give way to lingering yearns to spoon,
And starts the search for someone else.

When multiple differences destroy the rapture,
There's soon not much left to recapture;
Which often breaks the ties.

If it weren't for differences and non-compromise,
There'd be a lot more happiness, and much less demise,
Of the wonderful feelings of love.

Differences cause the generation gap,
When children rebel against adulthood and are zapped,
Into a world of their own and their peers.

If people would verbalize the differences seen,
And discover what real compromise means,
There'd be a lot more harmony,
And a shorter distance to the end of the rainbow.

BEGINNING OF THE END

I see the beginning of the end,
When man can't trust a friend.
If people don't stop and mend their ways,
We're sure to end our days.

I see much violence on the rise;
Much sorrow shows in many eyes.
If both young and old don't take control,
I fear they'll lose their souls.

When young folks start to take control,
And disrespect both young and old;
I fear the time can't be too far,
When the whole world is set ajar.

ROME WASN'T BUILT IN A DAY

Rome wasn't built in a day,
and Life's not served on a silver platter.
It always seems I've missed the boat,
And nothing I do seems to matter.

Each step I take seems a little bit higher,
Which makes it harder to climb.
My goals all seem to be out of reach,
And I always run out of time.

I just stopped to think of all that is past,
And all that is coming around;
And most certainly as I have lived through the past,
My strength steers me toward higher ground.

Rome wasn't built in a day, and it seems
That I'll not reach the goals set today;
But, I'll constantly try to move all stumbling blocks,
And God help those who stand in my way.

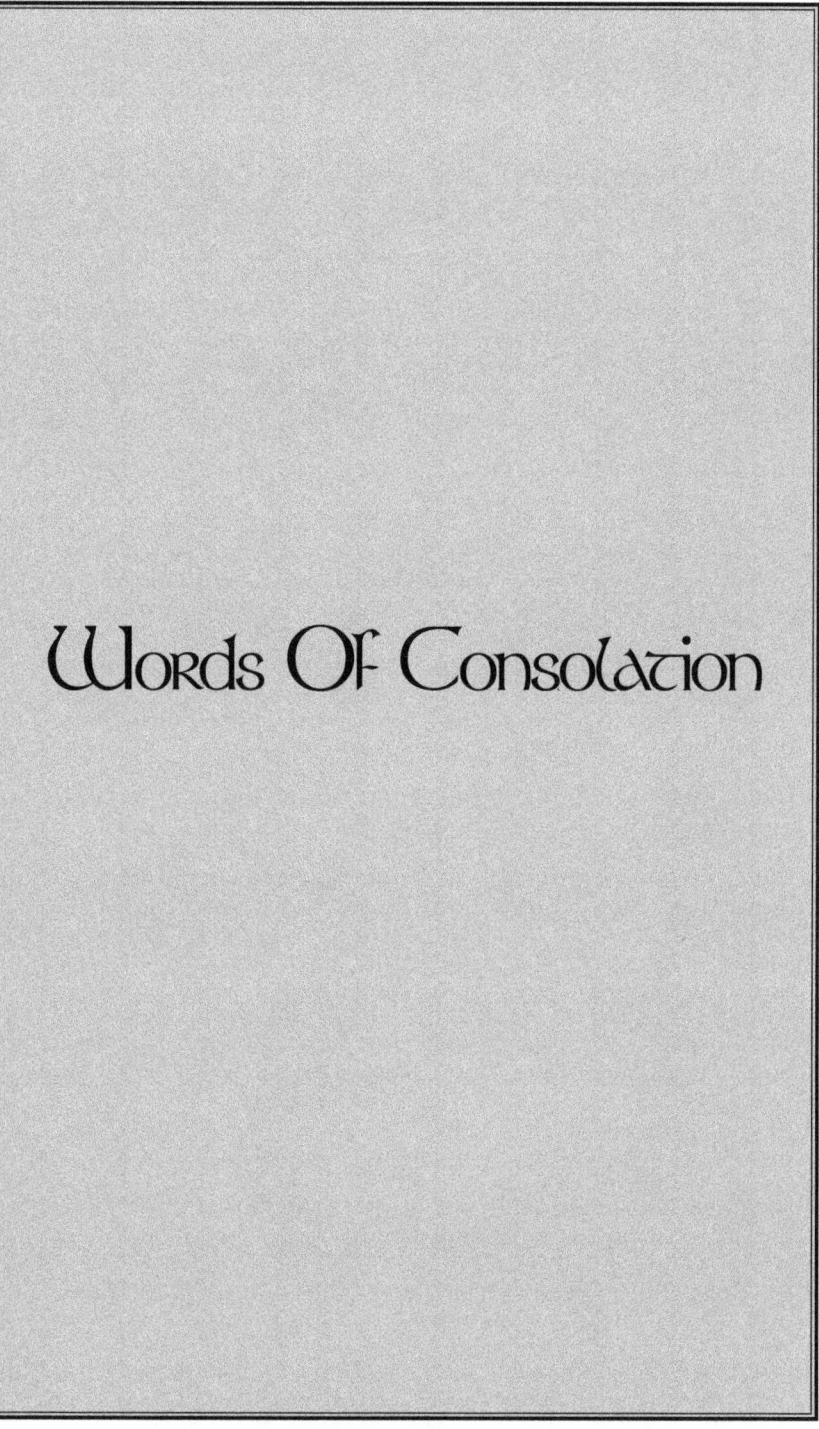

Words Of Consolation

PRAYER OF GUIDANCE

Oh Lord, please help me to,
Push on to a brighter day;
Forget about the past,
And trod on down life's highway.

Past tragedies still haunt me,
Till sleep I can not find.
My eyes are very weary;
My soul, for peace does pine.

The present time devours me;
My energy declines.
Oh Lord, put out the fire,
That keeps burning in my mind.

I know you're always with me;
I know your power divine.
I've witnessed your great love for me;
Your wishes are as mine.

Oh Lord, just give me strength,
To endure the pain I feel;
And guide my path with flowers,
While I follow at your heel.

FORGET ME NOT

Dear Lord, I know you promised,
That you would forget me not;
But still, sometimes I wonder,
If you possibly forgot.

You always let me linger,
Till I have no other out;
Or could this be my problem;
Finding what you're all about?

You always listen silently;
I know not if you're there;
But somehow you relieve me;
Your port, I know not where...

And sometimes when I suffer,
I fail to see your plot.
Dear Lord, I'm hoping you still care;
And you'll forget me not.

I'M GIFTED

I'm gifted with my hands and feet;
There are others who need help to eat.
There are those who never felt the earth,
Beneath their feet, ever since their birth.

I'm gifted with a mind that grows;
Each stage of life it somehow knows.
There are others born with minds so still;
With thoughts concealed against their will.

I'm gifted with two eyes that see;
There are others not as fortunate as me.
There are those who only smell the flowers;
Ne'r seen how high the palm tree towers.

Whenever I feel left out or used,
I remember the others who could not choose,
The path of which they wished to take;
The changes which they wished to make.

I'm gifted, in that I can see,
The things of which could hinder me;
And take the steps to change my course,
With help from HIS unearthly force.

THE POWER WITHIN ME

I can do most anything,
When I set my mind to do it.
With the grace of God and lots of faith,
All it takes is that I get to it.

I can climb the highest mountain,
Tame the most ferocious beast;
I don't need to ask of noone,
What to do, to say the least.

I've learned the power's within me,
To accomplish all my goals;
And that's also true of anyone,
So stop the ifs, ands, buts, and polls.

It took a long time for me to see,
That my power lies within my head.
If I would just believe in me,
My fears and woes, real soon I'll shed.

LET NOT YOUR HEART BE TROUBLED

Let not your heart be troubled;
For it need not be that way.
If you let *Him* know you trust *Him*,
He will guide you day by day.

He will comfort you and lead you,
No matter what odds may be.
Fear not that he'll deceive you,
Like earthly beings we see.

You must put forth *All* trust in *Him*,
And never have a doubt...
That *He* will do what's best for you,
And see your troubles out.

If you should stop to hesitate,
When deciding what to do;
That's proof you've failed to shift the weight,
To him instead of you.

So, let not your heart be troubled;
For you have someone who cares.
When others have abandoned you,
Remember... *He* is there.

IF I FORGET

Dear Lord, I know you hear me;
There's much I want to say.
Although I never see you;
You're with me every day.

There's something I'd like for you to know,
That I often do regret;
It's that my memory seems to fail...
Your powers I soon forget.

If I forget to call you when,
My burdens I can not bear;
Please don't forget to let me know,
That your presence is everywhere.

If I forget to thank you,
When you assist and take the wheel;
Please remember, I'm only human...
With human frailties by the reel.

If I forget to thank you,
For the things you did before;
Please jar my memory gently,
As you open door by door.

MY INTANGIBLE WEALTH

I may not be a scholar;
I may not be a star...
At least I have my head on straight;
I know I'm blessed by far.

I may not score one-hundred,
On any given test;
But, I've learned to use my head,
When deciding what is best.

Beauty can be just skin deep;
Or it can come from deep within;
So, I see a greater beauty,
In the face of a true friend.

Rags to riches is a dream,
That many people share...
But I have more than riches;
I have LOVE, and those who care.

INSIDE OUT

If only I could see within,
The things not shared without;
An open mind has always been,
What love is all about.

At times, when our love stands the test;
Your endurance seems to yield.
Those times are when I listen best,
To the inner thoughts you feel.

You feel as though you've reached a peak,
Where balance seems no more.
You've given way to self-defeat,
More often than before.

Our love can turn your inside out;
Diminish fears and woes.
Love conquers all, without a doubt;
And most of all... it grows.

LOVE

Love is like a whirlwind;
It comes suddenly and swift.
It confuses inner feelings;
Then sets your heart adrift.

Your life can be in a turmoil,
Or as peaceful as the calm of sea.
It can take on many shapes,
And create a jealousy.

It can place you in a world,
In which you wish to be;
A world of many fantasies,
With only you and he.

There will be some confusion;
Some heartaches and some bliss.
You'll even have some fears,
That his presence you will miss.

But Love can be a blessing too,
Which enhances self-control;
And motivates you endlessly,
Toward reaching all your goals.

TO LOVE IS...

To Love is... to know when to speak;
To know when our loved ones,
Our love does seek.

To Love is... to understand when,
To laugh, to smile, and sit a while,
With someone who cries out from within.

To Love is... not just a whim;
It's a feeling deep inside you,
For her or for him.

To Love is... to show deep affection;
To always be there,
For your loved ones' protection.

To Love is... to trust and feel free,
To confide and advise,
When problems you see.

To Love is... a mutual respect;
For one whom you cherish,
Which will never defect.

To Love is... forever;
In spite of our woes.
It's growing together,
As no one else knows.

FOREVER LOVE

You will find that Love is blind.
It sometimes tends to be unkind;
But, if it were not for love, I'm sure;
Life's hopes and dreams would be obscure.

A child interprets love to be,
Something you touch, and only see;
But love is something deep within;
It'll never tarnish, but will forever bend...

And though it seems as children grow;
The more love given, the less they show.
Love really has a great deal to do,
With what they feel, and how they grew...

And as adults we sometimes see,
The dark side of love, which can often be,
A test of true love... and devotion;
That LOVE IS FOREVER, and not a notion.

TRUE LOVE

True love is love unbound,
Which never ventures far.
It's when contentment's found,
In knowing how you are.

Though many see true love to be,
A kiss, a gift, a hug or two;
It means much more to me;
It's loving, caring, sharing with you.

True love can ne'r be haltered;
It thrives on being free.
Sometimes its course is altered,
When the other side we see.

Remember that true love still stands,
When infatuations die.
It even tends to hurt sometimes;
Sometimes you wonder... "Why?"

SECRET LOVE

If I should lay me down to sleep,
I dare not wink;
Instead I'd weep.

For I have seen beyond the door;
The whirlwind love,
Not seen before.

If I should try to close my eyes,
I dare not dream,
When my heart cries.

I gather all the strength I can,
To face myself...
And then my man.

And then I know I would survive,
The latent love,
Before my eyes.

FIRST LOVE

Oh love of loves, whom cupid claimed;
I dare not speak your name.
In my heart, you live forevermore;
In my head, sweet memories soar.

Oh love of loves, forever gone;
I wonder if you're now alone.
Your gentle touch, I reminisce;
Your loving ways, I often miss.

Oh love, sweet love, I'm hoping soon,
We'll meet again, beneath the moon.
A love like yours will be no more;
For you, my heart's an open door.

HOW SWEET

How sweet the smell
Of roses bright;
The morning mist;
The kiss of night.

How sweet the sound
Of humming bees;
A touch of wind
Among the trees.

How sweet the taste
Of cherry pie;
The gesture made
When friends come by.

How sweet the smell,
The sound, the taste;
How sweet the smile
Upon your face.

THE BIRTH OF NATURE

How swiftly does the wind blow;
So peaceful are the flowers;
How beautiful the rainbow;
So high the tree soon towers.

If I could ride upon the wind,
I'd venture far and near;
I'd drift among the tree tops,
And race with the fastest deer.

If I could be a flower;
Then peace I'd only find.
They come in great variety;
So, I'd be the colorful kind.

If I could be a rainbow,
I'd stretch across the nation;
And try to have all people see,
The beauty in HIS creation.

If I could be the tallest tree,
That ever grew on earth;
I'd stand steadfast and upright,
To symbolize nature's birth.

PEACE OF MIND

Dear Lord, I have but one request;
If you would be so kind.
Above all else, I'm asking that
You give me *Peace of Mind.*

Though many seek and treasure,
The material things they find;
There's nothing quite like having,
The much sought *Peace of Mind.*

If you will grant this one request,
All else would be inclined,
To fall according to your plan...
For peace at heart *and Mind.*

BURNT OUT

As I rise in the morning,
I wonder what's in store.
I wonder if the day will come,
When I will work no more.

I hear they say you get out,
Whatever you put in.
I wonder if the dam will break,
Before my ship comes in.

You know, I often wonder,
If what they say is true...
The harder that I seem to work;
The less the others do.

I wonder if my just reward
Is what I think you said.
You said I'd best be glad I have
A place to lay my head?

INGREDIENTS FOR A DOCTOR

A little bit of humanity;
A partial dose of tact;
An awful lot of patience,
A good doctor never lacks.

A dash of undying energy;
A lot of fresh concern;
An occasional ounce of sympathy,
For patients' stress unearned.

A lot of understanding;
An eye for obscure distress;
A bit of openmindedness,
Helps a patient's ills regress.

A DOCTOR

A doctor has no schedule...
For that I sympathize;
But constantly I thank the Lord,
For this angel in disguise.

I know not how you do it;
But most of all you care.
It means a lot, to say the least...
To know that you are there.

Though many patients tire you;
Show gratitude, so few...
You somehow seem to keep the faith;
And bring your patients through.

You take the time to listen;
And analyze my views.
You even go so far as write,
To those of whom I choose.

All this is still just part of you...
A doctor who deserves ado.
My many thanks go out to you;
My gratitude for what you do.

This poem is dedicated to Dr.'s Manual Myers and Arthur K. Huberman, of Kaiser Permanente Medical Group, Los Angeles, California.

A DOCTOR'S WIFE

It takes a lot of guts
To be a doctor's wife, you see.
There are no if's, and's, or but's
About how patient she must be.

She must look forward to the days,
When she must be alone;
Because a doctor's duties regulate,
The time he spends at home.

There's often some emergency,
To which he must attend;
A patient's life could be at stake;
His work day has no end.

Sometimes it seems to her as though,
His wife's concerns are last;
But when he reassures her,
These feelings quickly pass.

A doctor's wife contributes much,
To his strength and peace of mind.
He needs her love and her support...
And no better team you'll find.

This poem is dedicated to ALL doctors' wives.

GOOD FRIENDS ARE NICE TO HAVE

Good friends are nice to have...

When you wake up in the morning,
There's a smile upon your face.
You begin the day with kind thoughts,
And love for the human race.

You get up full of energy,
And off to work you go;
But as the day progresses,
Stress and tension seem to grow.

You look around for someone,
With a smile upon their face.
A friend is there to greet you,
Which helps to break the pace.

Your boss calls you in conference,
And the heat begins to rise.
In spite of all your efforts,
Your spirit slowly dies;
But, once again a friend steps in,
And relieves your inner cries...

Good Friends Are Nice To Have.

THIS JOB

Someday I'm gonna quit this job;
That day just might be soon.
If it weren't for the things I want,
I'd quit this afternoon.

If it were not for the bills that are due,
I'd tell the boss to shove it.
If it were not for high prices too,
I wouldn't act as if I love it.

If it were not for my family,
I'd just roam and work at will;
But, until the kids have all grown up,
I guess I'll just keep still.

ANXIETY

I don't want to be remembered,
For the evil deeds I've done.
I don't want to be forgotten,
In the presence of someone.

I don't want to be resented,
By the very ones I love.
I don't want to be presented,
With the wrath of God above.

I just want to make impressions,
Upon the people I adore.
I just want to give concessions,
To the friends I have no more.

I just want to find the person,
That is locked up deep inside.
I just want to ease the burden,
Of the things I try to hide.

I'M ONLY HUMAN

I am not invincible;
Nor am I perfect in every sense.
I'm not even deemed infallible;
Must live life at my expense.

I'm not lacking in emotions;
Can't be programmed not to fail.
I've a very rapid heartbeat;
A physique that's sometimes frail.

My memory sometimes fails me,
And sometimes I lose control.
After all, I'm only human,
With a human heart and soul.

CAN'T QUIT

One, two, three, four;
What on earth am I working for?

I come home every payday,
With my check held in my hand.
I proceed to make deposit,
Due to creditors' demands.

I say I'm going to save somehow;
Yet, still I know not when.
Someday I'm going to take a trip;
Someday I'm going to win.

The bills are all a toss-up;
Can't seem to bring them down.
Sometimes I entertain the thought...
"Oh Heck, I'll just leave town".

And then there's Uncle Sam,
Who takes a portion of my pay.
There's no method to his madness;
Not a darn thing I can say.

What Uncle Sam and bills don't take,
Utilities exhaust;
Household expense... and then there's rent;
Can't quit at any cost.

LIFE IS A BATTLEFIELD

Life is a battlefield,
And causes we have many.
If we should stop to clear debris,
We're bound to find not any.

Life is a battlefield,
Where people fight to win.
They fight for rights, they fight for life;
And often do give in.

Life is a battlefield;
In wars we do defend;
But when things get tough for us,
We seem to have no wind.

Life is a battlefield,
Of which we all are prey;
But the battle's never quite as hard,
When you let God lead the way.

IF I'M TO WIN THE RACE

Lord, I've got to be much stronger,
If I'm to win this race;
Can't hold on too much longer...
Won't quit, and can't keep pace.

I've moved a many stumbling blocks;
Trod a many rocky road.
I need your strength to carry on;
Your grace to lighten my load.

I can't depend or trust no one,
In this world to which I'm bound.
I've yet to falter or to rest;
By your grace I'll not fall down.

So help me Lord, to be much stronger;
I'm weary, weak, and worn.
My hands are bound; my feet stand still;
My tattered soul is torn.

Lead not me to temptation,
To join those of whom I see;
Instead, extend thy hand toward earth;
Make a pillar of stone of me.

THE LIFE MY FATHER GAVE

I couldn't ask for anything better,
Than the life my FATHER gave.
He gave me faith, strength and endurance,
Which I will carry to my grave.

He taught me how to love, in spite of,
The evil deeds to me outcast.
My faith has always reassured me,
I'd have the strength to always last.

He gave me sight to see beyond,
The exterior of all men;
To see and feel their inner thoughts;
And silent words to comprehend.

He gave me patience to await the things,
Which I am sure will come to me;
And in the event those things don't come;
He gave me the sense to set them free.

I'm quite fortunate to have these gifts,
Of which so many fail to see.
I thank my *Father* for his good grace,
And for all he's been to me.

MY TIME HAS COME

To you, my leaving's sad;
But to me, my time has come.
The world's so full of hatred,
And my job on earth is done.

Yield not to pain and sorrow,
Behind my leaving you this way.
Just be glad my soul's at peace,
And listen to the things I say.

Though evil often greets you,
Resist the fears and thoughts of woe.
In this world of sin and sorrow,
You'll need more grace than you will know.

And most of all, be happy,
As you live life day by day;
Because the happiness you feel,
Again, may never come your way.

Whatever does go wrong,
To turn your life's dreams upside down;
Don't forget, you're not alone;
For God will always be around.

QUITE OFTEN WE FORGET

Quite often we forget the many homeless in the street,
And quite frequently we gouge on all the food we have to eat;
Never think about the ones who never have a shoe to wear;
It more often seems as though for them, we very seldom care.

It's quite often that we visit the market in the neighborhood;
Never think about the ones who very often wished they could.
We still take a lot for granted, as we venture day by day;
While the poor, weak and deprived... suffer, die, or waste away.

Now it's time to show compassion for the poor and homeless people,
Reach down into our hearts and help to be our brothers' keepers.
Through the gifts we give today, some will flourish and rejoice;
And some others will be lifted, as our songs of love be voiced.

Though so many softly spoken, peer from shelters they call home;
We can not leave them there... to suffer life's bad spills alone.
If we just take a hand and nurture weakness back to health,
We'll find love more rewarding than the most abundant wealth.

SOMEONE ELSE

I can make my face to look like someone else;
    But it's not really me you see.

I can learn to walk and talk like someone else;
    But I'd rather walk and talk like me.

I can learn to do what others do quite well;
But then there'd be no difference you could tell.

I can change my views, to keep your faith in me;
But I don't think that's the way it's meant to be.

I can make myself a clone of those whom you desire;
But then my self-respect would very soon retire.

I can do all of these things, and put you to the test;
Then, "Guess What?" ...
You'll find it's me that you love best.

Someone Else

ABOUT THE AUTHOR

Mary was born in Osceola, Arkansas. She was raised in Cleveland, Ohio, from the age of 5 to 18 years of age. She then moved to Los Angeles, California, where she currently resides.

From the very young age of 16, Mary realized the necessity to apply herself whole-heartedly toward reaching the goals which she had set for her life. She began to educate herself, in addition to the public education which she received. However, it was still not until much later in life that she was constantly made aware of the need to educate and assist others in special areas of concern to most of us.

Mary's work experience background includes approximately 15 years in a Government agency. Her prolific qualities allowed her to become proficient in the duties of a vast variety of positions held and that she was temporarily placed in during her employment years. Like a sponge, she acquired numerous skills with ease, and received numerous awards for her proficiency. Not only did she have administrative skills; but she has artistic talents as well. Her love for writing, photography, and poetry led her to a new path in life.

It is a fact that we all are striving to survive and succeed in all of our endeavors, whatever they may be. Mary purposely acquired all of the knowledge and experience that she had in order to meet her goals, and to help others to meet their's. She has been a philanthropist, as well as an achiever, since early childhood. She feels that anything can be achieved, if you set your mind to it. Her recognition of the fallacy of bound failure in others caused her to have the desire to make changes where possible.

Mary began to develop her artistic talents after she went to California, following her marriage. She began oil painting without training or education. She later took an oil painting class, and a correspondence course in Commercial Art. Photography became her interest after her marriage. She began entering photo contests and taking family portraits, as well as nature scenes. Her photography was recognized in the Photographer's Forum Magazine Annual edition, in 1986. She later developed numerous other uses for her photography and artistic skills.

Mary's writing career began in 1982. Since then, she has written one book, completed the poetry originals and photography for her own Greeting Card business; has a selection of photography and poetry for wall plaques and prints; has written some song lyrics. Mary feels that with her educational, experience background, and artistic abilities, she has much to offer to the public. Therefore, this book is the first effort to reach out and touch, and influence many people's lives in a positive way; and to share her knowledge and perception of life with others. She hopes the reader not only enjoys the contents; but will also benefit by enrichment of their current and future life.

ABOUT THE BOOK

This book developed as result of compilation of numerous individual poems of life. Mary first began writing poetry as a hobby, after her unfortunate disability from her job. She found that writing was very consoling, due to the fact that it allows free expression of emotions, thoughts, and concerns. At first there were only a few poems; then more… and more; until there were enough to be put into a book format. Once it was decided to combine her poetry into a book, she thought carefully about the format and flow of the book. There were enough poems in several different categories to create titled sections.

Mary began with a collection of poems which addresses CHANGING TIMES. It was very easy for help to reflect upon this category because she has witnessed the changing of our times from the past through several generations, from the East coast to the West Coast. She has seen the mounting stresses in the lives of our next generation of adults.

The next category chosen was PERILS OF LIFE. The poems contained in this section of the book depict the many perils of life that our young people are experiencing in their struggle to survive and be counted. She has come to realize that these perils of life are the downfall of many of our youths and young adults. She also sees that the lack of the ability to endure and resolve the effects of these same perils has caused many of our young people to move in directions that sometimes end in no return to a normal healthy lifestyle.

The third category: WORD TO THE WISE, contains poetry pertaining to many elements in life which are reflected in the actions and emotions of many people today. They address the elements in all stages of life, which cause us not to develop strong minds and relationship with the people we are close to, and the ones we interact with daily. These poems are also intended to be thought-provoking. They offer ways of getting to the root of problems, in order to clear the path for healing. They also force the reader to be honest with his or herself.

Last, but not the least is: WORDS OF CONSOLATION, which contains many poems of love, some humor, and self-gratification. Mary felt that these poems were much needed, to round the flow of the book off, because she knows well that all individuals need some pleasure in life to balance the negative occurrences and emotions. Love is what keeps us going; whether it be for a parent, a friend, another family member, a spouse, or a girl-friend or boyfriend. She saved this for last, because she wishes that to be the last and utmost thing on the reader's mind… "Keep love in your heart", and everything else will follow accordingly. Another important thing is, to keep an open mind. Closed minds will stunt your emotional growth. Mary hopes that all readers of this book will learn to live, endure and resolve the problems in their lives with the thoughts in this book in mind.

CPSIA information can be obtained
at www.ICGtesting.com
Printed in the USA
LVHW020401140420
653368LV00002B/373